I0210130

Reading People:

Harness the Power Of Personality, Body Language, Influence and Persuasion To Transform Your Work, Relationships & Boost Your Confidence!

Copyright Notice

No part of this book may be reproduced or transmitted in any form whatsoever, electronic, or mechanical, including photocopying, recording, or by any information storage or retrieval system without expressed written, dated and signed permission from the author. All copyrights are reserved.

Disclaimer

Reasonable care has been taken to ensure that the information presented in this book is accurate. However, the reader should understand that the information provided does not constitute legal, medical or professional advice of any kind.

No Liability: this product is supplied "as is" and without warranties. All warranties, express or implied, are hereby disclaimed. Use of this product constitutes acceptance of the "No Liability" policy. If you do not agree with this policy, you are not permitted to use or distribute this product.

We shall not be liable for any losses or damages whatsoever (including, without limitation, consequential loss or damage) directly or indirectly arising from the use of this product.

Claim This Now

The Confident New You - Develop Your Confidence and Start Living the Life You Deserve

Do you get lost for words around other people, or do you suffer from social anxiety?

If your confidence is always holding you back from achieving what you really want in your life, or if you have always been super shy with no confidence then read on.

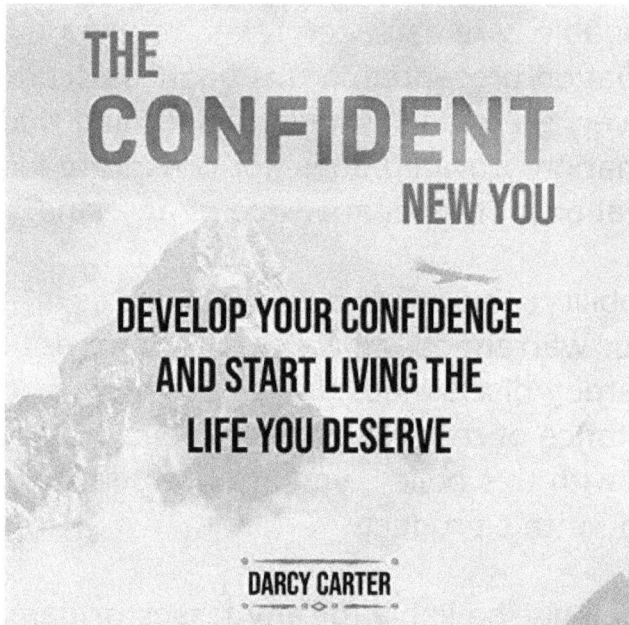

THE
CONFIDENT
NEW YOU

**DEVELOP YOUR CONFIDENCE
AND START LIVING THE
LIFE YOU DESERVE**

DARCY CARTER

Introduction

Imagine a life where you can easily read people. Where you can tell if someone is having a negative or a positive effect on you. Or if they really like you or not? Imagine the value your life would receive if you could discover when someone was lying to you. Or if they really had your best interests in mind.

Think about how such an ability could help you excel in life. Imagine if after meeting someone you could gain real insights into their true personality to find out what type of person they really are. In fact you could even use this knowledge to take a look at your own personality to see what it might reveal about you.

Reading people is a powerful way to realize people's intentions, figure out who is sincere, manage relationships and much more. The ability to quickly read a person gives us a massive advantage in business, love and life. These abilities might seem like they're straight out of a superhero movie. But the truth is that with the right knowledge you can get a glimpse into a person's mind and know what they're really thinking.

Every second of every day, everybody around you is broadcasting a signal. Your ability to read other people depends on how well you're able to read those signals. It is a skill that you can use to improve every area of your life. With enough practice reading people quickly and effectively will become more natural for you.

The first thing you need to do in learning how to read people is to become more self aware. That is, you have to be aware of when you form opinions about other people. At a certain point, between meeting a stranger, and then interacting with them you will start to form an opinion of them. That could be, "I just don't trust this person". Or "This person is really cool" and so on. The truth is, only a few minutes have passed. You aren't aware of their history and don't know much about them. Whatever they say could be real, lies, or otherwise. Intuition is what you are tuning into. When you get good at noticing how you feel about people you become better at picking up on clues and reading people.

Reading people involves listening, observing and then understanding. Every person gives away clues all the time and everyone has individual personalities. Always be on the lookout for them. During every interaction you should be collecting information and summarizing it. Then you can calibrate your demeanor and communication to suit them and the result will be higher quality interactions.

When you start reading people begin with an open mind. Approach all of your interactions with a blank slate and no judgement. You can start out with small talk to familiarize yourselves. Whilst some people are confident and outgoing there are others who will be more reserved and shy. When you come across shy people they might seem a little antisocial or standoffish. However don't take it personally just go slowly and get them talking. Let them know you are friendly by smiling at them. It doesn't matter if they smile back or not, take the first step. Smiling will send them a positive first message about yourself.

Always make the first move. You can then introduce yourself and have a topic ready to get things rolling. You could bring up a funny story or something situational such as the setting your in or a movie you watched recently and so on. Taking the initiative will take the pressure off them. At the outset you should speak for eighty percent of the time. Avoid asking too many questions early on and try just to keep talking.

When it comes to asking questions go with open ended questions. You want to elicit the most informational responses that keep conversations going. Closed ended questions that elicit yes or no responses will stop the conversation. Focus on questions with, how, what, when, why, or who in them. At the start conversations light and cordial. If you want to go deeper then you can try revealing weaknesses of yours. This will make people more comfortable with you and more likely to open up information to you.

Listen actively, this means really tuning into what people are saying and showing interest in it. Shy people will be more sensitive so show some empathy to them. Repeat what they and try to summarize the points, then follow up with deeper questioning. Avoid interrupting or dominating the chat. Try to resist any of that. If there is silence be comfortable with that and give them the opportunity to fill it. Sometimes shy people will be hesitant to speak and you may need to give them more time.

Monitor how engaged they are. Tell tale signs are their level of eye contact and how much they speak. If they don't show much eye contact or only reply with short answers then you need to work on better engagement with them. Stick with the subjects they like and drill deeper into those subjects with more open ended conversations.

If they really aren't interested just smile and move on. Always be gracious and polite. On the other hand if you had a good conversation you can invite the person out again. From there you can develop a relationship. Exchange contact information and set ip something low pressure such as after work drinks. Or if your conversations were on activities and hobbies you could lead that into going to do those things.

Remember that when you are reading people try to be subtle about it. Many people might become defensive if you are being over analytical of them. Ideally you should observe others without them knowing about it which will produce the most accurate readings.

How you spend your time will affect your ability to read people. If you spend long periods of time alone or working on computers then it's going to be more difficult to read people. That also includes excessive use of smart phones, tablets and so on.

To begin reading people we must understand personality.

Part One: Personality

Have you ever wondered why people behave a certain way or why they react in different ways? Have you ever wished to understand someone better? Or how to get along with people at work?

The way we react and behave is different from others because we all have our own desires, fears and individual personalities. We are motivated by our thoughts and our actions are the result.

When you understand yourself and the people around you it will improve your professional and personal relationships. Knowing a person's personality type will improve your interactions. In addition this will remove any pre judgements or first impressions.

In the following chapters we will explore various personality measuring tools and types to help you read people.

The Big Five Personality Traits

Personality is a massive influence on the way that a person reacts to various situations. Psychologists have identified five traits of personality that describe the character of a person. These personality traits influence behaviour, relationships, career path, lifestyle and more. They are a key indicator in reading people.

Each person will have their own characteristic personality traits that will prevail throughout their life. Typically one trait will be more dominant in certain people. The dynamics of someone's family, their relationships and upbring will also affect these traits. Research points towards nurture being accountable to half of the influence whilst the other half depends on their environments. From childhood to adulthood personality tends to remain relatively stable.

The big five traits of personality are, extroversion, openness, conscientiousness, neuroticism and agreeableness. When you are interacting with people look out for these characteristics.

Let's take a look at them in more depth.

Openness

High Score	Low Score
• Enjoy trying new things	• Dislikes change
• Creative	• Traditional thinking
• Enjoy challenges	• Not very imaginative
• Good imagination	• Dislikes theoretical concepts

People with high levels of openness are more open minded and receptive to new ideas. They are adventurous, like to be challenged and enjoy experiencing new things. High scorers in openness are creative and inquisitive to learn new things that enhance their knowledge. Low scorers tend to be more conservative. They dislike anything foreign or unfamiliar but are quite efficient. However a mixture of high and low levels of openness can be useful depending on the situation. People high in openness tend to do well in creative pursuits such as science and the arts. Those having lower levels of openness tend to work well in accounting, law and sales.

Conscientiousness

High Score	Low Score

• Orderly	• Less organized
• Goal driven	• Procrastinates
• Pays attention to detail	• Impulsive
• Persistent	• Messy

Discipline and dutifulness are two important aspects of the conscientiousness personality. High scorers are well organized, hard-working, self disciplined and efficient. They are goal driven, perfectionists who tend to be workaholics. This manifest in their life, for instance with clean and well organized homes. On the other hand people low in conscientiousness can be seen as more spontaneous and playful. They find it hard to motivate themselves and are often unorganized.

People high in conscientiousness tend to do well in jobs that allow for planning and goal setting such as executive roles or sales. Whilst those having lower levels of conscientiousness tend to work well in less structured roles such as freelancing or independent business.

Extraversion

High Score	Low Score
• Make friends easily	• Worn out after

	socializing
• Energized by other people	• Dislikes small talk
• Says things before thinking	• Prefers solitude
• Seeks excitement or adventure	• Difficult to start conversations

High scorers in extraversion are outgoing, assertive, cheerful and enjoy social interactions. This has a significant impact on social behavior which results in strong social skills and an active social calendar. On the other hand they are extremely uncomfortable spending time alone. Low scorers in extraversion are more reserved, quiet and prefer more time alone. That does not necessarily mean they are antisocial but typically require less stimulation and may become easily worn out in social activities.

People high in extraversion tend to do well in roles that involve engaging with people such as teaching, politics and sales. Whilst those having lower levels of extraversion tend to work well in less public roles such as writing or the arts.

Agreeableness

High Score	Low Score
• Always ready to help	• Stubborn
• Feels empathy for others	• Insults and belittles others
• Interested in others	• Manipulative
• Caring and honest	• Self-centered

High scorers in agreeableness are kind, altruistic and tolerant. Getting along with others is important to them and thus they are flexible and reluctant to criticize or judge people. Politeness and compassion are the hallmarks of people with this personality trait. They are good hearted people who are extremely cooperative, empathetic and trustworthy. However, agreeableness is not useful in situations requiring tough or objective decisions.

People low in agreeableness tend to be skeptical, argumentative, selfish and blunt. They also are defensive of their beliefs and can sometimes be overly judgemental of others.

People high in agreeableness tend to make great leaders in companies, politics and education. Whilst those having lower levels of agreeableness do well in workplaces where they need to make hard decisions and deliver bad news such as managerial roles.

Neuroticism

High Score	Low Score
• Stressed easily	• Calm in stressful situations
• Worries about many things	• Optimistic
• Easily upset	• Emotionally stable
• Mood swings	• Rarely feels sad or depressed

People high in neuroticism are usually emotionally unstable and get upset easily. Often a person who is moody, worries about things and gets irritated or nervous frequently. Managing stress is a challenge for them and they easily succumb to negative moods. Studies conclude that dominance in this personality trait makes a person more susceptible to depression.

On the other side, low scorers in neuroticism are more calm and less likely to worry. Thus being low in neuroticism may be considered to be an advantage.

However it can make people too careless and likely to downplay potential threats.

People who are higher in neuroticism tend to work well in safe and secure environments that allow them creative space such as design and writing. Whilst those having lower levels of neuroticism tend to thrive in environments that utilize their composed temperament. Potential job ideas are, law and psychiatry.

Introverts and Extroverts

An easy way to read people is to find out if a person is introverted or extroverted. Once you understand how this works you can improve your interactions with others.

The late 20th-century Swiss psychiatrist Carl Jung popularized the use of introvert and extrovert personality types to help with understanding the various attitudes and behaviors of his patients.

Introverts are people whose attention and focus is usually directed inwards to their thoughts and feelings. Whereas an extrovert's are people whose attention is directed more towards the external world and other people.

Although we have dominant characteristics, these are not necessarily fixed. People also adapt their personality in different situations and with different people. For example an introvert working in a job that requires extroversion may decide to be more social because it's important for their career development. Or, for example an extrovert who is leading a team might decide to take time out from giving orders to instead listen to staff.

So what can we learn about ourselves when we understand which side of the personality fence we are sitting on? And how does this influence our career choices, relationships and overall lifestyle?

Extroverts

An extrovert is usually the first to speak up. If you ask a question and the person immediately responds and seems to be thinking out loud. Then there is a good chance that they have an extroverted personality. If after asking a question the person takes a second or two to respond. Then there is a good chance that they have an introverted personality type.

Human connection has a greater influence on extroverts than introverts. In fact, it has been proven that the brains of extroverts respond more to photos of humans faces than compared to neutral photos of nature. An extrovert will confide in anyone, they speak more and often have a big circle of friends. However the connections are not particularly strong.

In working environments extroverts perform well in careers involving direct interaction with people and team based efforts. They enjoy working in open spaces, are quick decision makers and enjoy lots of attention. However they are easily distracted. Some examples are of jobs perfect for extraverts are events, police officer, musician and entertainer.

One of the most famous extraverts is Bill Clinton. The former President of the United States of America was always full of energy. Clinton thrived in publicity and energized people through speeches and meetings. To both friends and opponents he will be remembered as, outgoing, social and friendly.

Then we have the famous martial artist, Connor Mcgregor. He calls himself the notorious, the two time champ. He is as famous for his public persona as well as his fighting skills. Mcgregor is a prime example of an extrovert, taunting his opponents with lively rhetoric, as much as his brutal fighting skills. He is flamboyant in the ring, always a showman, and in interviews he is never shy.

Then there is the former British Prime Minister Winston Churchill who had an endless energy, working all hours fueled by whiskey and cigars. Even when he was leading a country at war, he also found energy to write a Nobel Prize winning memoir.

Introverts

Introverts are usually quiet and reserved. They are considered to be more reflective, thinkers who are happy in long periods of solitude. To identify an introvert observe how they recover when stressed or tired. This is a key difference between extroverts and introverts. Introverts tend to withdraw into isolation and sit alone in order to recharge their energy. The more time spent around people in particular large groups of acquaintances will drain their energy. In addition they may also find things such as external noise distracting and will prefer total silence when working. An introvert may only share ideas when prompted.

Age is also a great indicator for reading if someone is introverted or extroverted. As we grow older we tend to calm down and go to more moderate social engagements that require less extroversion.

Brain scans show a more developed prefrontal cortex in introverts which is associated with deeper thinking and planning. This suggests that introverts are less impulsive and prefer to think things over before taking action. However this kind of overthinking makes them more susceptible to depression and anxiety.

Introverts tend to prefer more deep conversation and appreciate listening to others. Give them plenty of space during conversations and respect their time. They will want to know that they are being understood. If they feel your not interested in what they have to say then they will likely leave. If you want to make a real connection with them then listen with care and interest. Also be sure to respond authentically and in depth. If you're an extrovert talking to an introvert make sure to give them enough time to respond after you say something.

All of this doesn't mean to say that introverts are antisocial. They will often appreciate being in contact with others. It just depends on with whom and for how long. Introverts are just as capable as extroverts of applying social skills. They will likely manage their interactions in a more disciplined way with a defined schedule. Its less likely for them to indulge in social activities as a form of escapism. Time is also an important factor in the decision making process of introverts. Often pressuring them for a decision is a bad strategy. Introverts will make their best decisions with time and solitude.

Jobs that allow a person to working independently are a good fit for introverts. Introverts prefer working in quiet spaces and don't need praise. They tend to ponder decision-making more carefully and are good at focusing for long periods of time. Ideal jobs for introverts include, graphic design, software development, taxi driver and more.

On of the famous introverts is Bill Gates, the founder of technology giant Microsoft. He is well known for being incredibly focused which has allowed him to spend thousands of working on complicated tasks. He has talked about having to learn some extravert skills due to the demands of running such a huge company.

Perhaps one of the most surprising introverts is Michael Jordan. You might think that sports is all about being extroverted. But Jordan was well known for being reclusive. Preferring to spend long periods of time alone recharging and perfecting his game.

Then there is Facebook founder and CEO Mark Zuckerberg. He is known as being shy and introverted. To people that don't know him he comes off as cold and reserved. But he does genuinely care about the people working with him and excels working for long periods of time alone.

What about relationships, is there an ideal match up?

Often it's difficult for extroverts to truly understand introverts. Conflict could be caused because the extrovert wishes to go out and be social whereas the introvert will likely prefer to stay home. Extroverts may become upset with their partner for being antisocial and not talking with people. The extrovert may well encourage the introvert socialize, but this might be perceived as being too pushy and not accepting them. The introvert may feel that the extrovert never listens and speaks too much.

There are clearly many differences between introverts and extroverts. Being an introvert or extrovert is neither better or worse than the other. Most people have both aspects integrated into their personality and sit naturally between the two. They are commonly known as ambiverts who have a personality type that doesn't lean heavily in either direction. As a result they have a much easier time adjusting to various situations which helps them to connect more easily with a wider variety of people.

The Masks People Wear

People wear masks to hide their real identity, emotions and feelings. The world can be a tough place and a natural response is to hide behind a mask. Social pressure, abuse and harassment cause people to mask their normal personality. This can be at the cause of strong influences such as parents, rejection and physical or emotional abuse. Sometimes the habit of wearing a mask runs so deep that the individual might not even be aware of their masking.

Many of us wear masks in our career, others in socializing or daily living and so on. A person could be feeling terrible on the inside but hide it with a big smile. Sometimes we feel obligated to wear a mask because you have to hide the truth from others. This is really commonplace in work and environments with hierarchy.

People go to great lengths to attain social acceptance. Pretending to be confident. Faking humour, gossiping and so on. Sometimes when we are insecure we might lie and make things up. Or when we don't feel loved we can mask that with anger. We pretend things are fine, even when they are not.

Many of us hide who we truly are through these masks. We hide from our loved ones and ultimately from ourselves. Some people have put on so many masks that they have lost themselves and the essence of who they truly are.

A lot of these behaviors are the result of our childhood experiences that later shape us. Not many of us emerge from childhood with a fresh attitude. We unconsciously and consciously adopt certain behavioural patterns to seek stability and security in our lives. These are our masks and protect us from shame and hurt. Here are some of the masks we wear.

Avoidance Mask

Sensitive individuals and sufferers of anxiety often try to hide their real self behind an avoidance mask to avoid all the pain. Imposter syndrome is one of the most common reasons for wearing masks. We fear that everyone is going to find us out. They are going to find out that all along we are a fake. But being yourself without that mask is fine. We need to live into our potential.

Functional Mask

A Functional Mask is the type people wear at work to look competent. Consider famous people who don't want to show their emotions to the tabloids as an example. In this regard you still feel your emotions but shield them from others temporarily.

Mask of Anger

Anger can be a protection mechanism to avoid getting hurt. Angry people often cover up their sensitivities in this way. On the other hand some might mask that with happiness. Joking and smiling all the time to hide their anxieties and insecurity.

The Calm

Looking from the outside this person appears to be calm and collected in all situations. Conflicts and chaos don't rattle them. But behind the mask they bottle up emotions which often boil over into nervous breakdowns and snapping at people.

The Humorist

Humour is a powerful defense mechanism. However it does prevent intimacy. Especially sarcasm which is usually rooted in pain. The humorist tends to avoid serious conversations by cracking jokes and will be uncomfortable with conflict. Their comedy serves as a protective shield.

The Overachiever

Some strive to achieve perfectionism as a defense mechanism against their world falling apart. Accolades and praise may provide some temporary relief but they are always at the mercy of things going wrong. The result is that the are in a perpetual state of anxiety. In addition the associated stubbornness and obsessiveness makes it difficult for them to build trust and intimacy with loved ones.

The Martyr

The Martyr believes they have a critical role in the world and rationalizes their selfless actions in this regard. These exaggerations often drive people away.

The Bully

Most of us are familiar with bullies. From the schoolyard to the workplace we often encounter the bully. The bully will try to assert control over others from gentle manipulation to more aggressive or even physical intimidation. Bullies may appear to be confident and powerful but their manipulation often stems from insecurities and self doubt. They feel the need to demand respect as a way of gaining value.

The Control Freak

Control freaks are fearful of ambiguity. They use order and exertion of power in an attempt to achieve a sense of security. They are usually over caring for all of those around them even when they are quite fine. When others deviate from plans they become agitated.

Self Loathing

Self loathing individuals project a negative view of themselves and are at the mercy of their own insecurities. This makes it difficult for them to be intimate with others. In some ways they see this as a protective mechanism from getting hurt.

The People Pleaser

People pleasers have their sense of value based on the opinion of others and will go to great lengths to win approval from them. They lack a strong foundation and will seek advice from others. They are also easily influenced by the opinions of others and will do whatever it takes to make others happy. Their own preferences, thoughts or feelings are suppressed as a result.

The Introvert

Introverts would much rather be lonely then risk failure or rejection. Just like the perfectionist they are afraid of making mistakes so avoid challenges. They are embarrassed easily and avoid saying much in order to avoid being wrong.

The Social Butterfly/Extravert

Social butterflies might appear to be the life and soul of the party but they are often lonely and empty on the inside. They compensate for their feelings of insecurity with small talk and fleeting experiences. Often they will have many people around them and a busy social calendar but most of those so called friendships are lacking in depth. Conversations are kept superficial to avoid revealing anxieties. Relationships are also shallow and promiscuity is common.

The Myers-Briggs Type, Indicator (MBTI)

The Myers-Briggs Type, Indicator (MBTI) is an excellent tool for reading people and understanding relationships. MBTI explains cognition which is how people process information. These are the four basic modes of cognition that every person has. Those are sensing, intuition, thinking and feeling. These four modes also exist in two orientations either introverted or extroverted and these combinations form the eight cognitive functions.

Note that extraverted used with these terms means anything happening external to your mind. This is in the real world, in real time. When you see the word introverted it means what goes on on the inside. That can be past present or future.

The human brain takes in information through perceiving and then makes decisions through judging. Perceiving is the process of taking in information from the external world and compiling it in our minds. Judging is the process of evaluating that information based on either internal or external criteria.

When you understand about cognitive functions and personality types it will help you to read people.

Perceiving Functions

There are four ways to take in information which are known as perceiving functions. Those are:

Extraverted Sensing (Se):
spontaneous, adaptable, optimistic and adventurous

Extroverted sensing involves experiencing the world around you in the form of sights, sounds and sensations. The process happens in the present moment. Extroverted sensors tend to notice much more details and respond faster than others. They also learn very quickly from experiences. They excel at noticing data from experiences and then making practical use of the knowledge. They also seek to understand the world around them and participate in it. As such they are energized from direct interaction with the outside world such as people, nature and events.

Introverted Sensing (Si):
Reliable, routine, clear and attentive

Introverted sensors draw on past experiences to understand the present and future. They pay close attention to detail and use this to quickly problem solve and make decisions. Sensing introverted involves remembering experiences in detail and comparing them to other experiences to in turn find similarities. These are individuals who are focused on their inner, subjective world of personal experiences.

They tend to have a strong intuition, self regulation and awareness. This makes them great at coming up with solutions. In their personal lives they prefer consistency and loyalty. As a result they often will have the same set of friends or relationships for their life.

Extraverted Intuiting (Ne):
Inspiring, impatient, imaginative, charismatic

Extraverted Intuitors are good at identifying relationships between things and finding hidden meanings behind things. They view everything as being connected and having many possibilities. However living in a world of multiple possibilities can make them unsure of their conclusions or cause them to have trouble deciding. Primarily they tend to be focused on the future and seeing the bigger picture. To many they are inspiring but often get stuck in the monotony of day to day life. They like to express new ideas and possibilities with great enthusiasm, often jumping from ideas. This makes them great entrepreneurs since they prefer to innovate and work well in chaos.

Introverted Intuiting (Ni):
Individualistic, strategic, mysterious, creative

Introverted intuitors are very good at noticing patterns, relationships between things and how they fit into a larger picture. They tend to find meaning in abstract concepts. As a result they are great at solving problems and planning for the future. They are always looking forward to the future and are less concerned with present circumstances. Primarily they are focused on their inner subjective world which they seek to connect with the outer world. They tend to work well withdrawn from external stimulation and can be quite unpredictable but very insightful. Often they will seem very detached from their environment and come across as daydreamers. For them it is difficult to explain their insights and they are often slow to reply because they get frustrated when explaining themselves. Abstract art or music are better ways for them to explain.

Judging Functions

There are four ways we make decisions which are known as judging functions. We use the judging functions when making decisions. Remember, everyone uses both thinking and feeling, but some prioritize one over the other. Those are:

Extraverted Thinking (Te):
leader, attention to detail, confident, strict

Extraverted thinkers are very good at organizing and efficiency. When they decide to accomplish a goal they're very good at finding potentially successful solutions. They may come off as authoritative but in reality they are trying to do there best to make things work. Primarily they focus on logical judgments to organize and evaluate information in the outer world.

Emotionally they might seem detached since they are more logical. Ambiguity and indecisiveness frustrate them. In some cases they might rush into decisions too quickly because they want results and are highly goal orientated. Often found working in law, politics and planning.

Introverted Thinking (Ti):
Analytical, honest, smart, logical

Introverted thinking involves organizing, analyzing and evaluating to complete a bigger picture or to better understand things. Introverted thinkers are energized by challenges and troubleshooting. They tend to make decisions based on an internal framework which they are constantly revising and expanding on. Once something has been analyzed and evaluated they will trust in it. As a result they seek perfection and internal order. However they are less likely to share the logic behind when they make a decision and instead prefer privacy. Often they are critical of others and can come across as judgemental. They often look for inconsistencies or flaws mentally try to improve things to reach the best of all possibilities.

Extraverted Feeling (Fe):
Kind, empathetic, sensitive, sincere

Extraverted Feelers focus on the feelings and intentions of other people around them. They are focused on decisions that add value to the

environment, social standards and culture.
Considerate of others and will often put them ahead of themselves. Their primary motivation is to understand the values and desires of other people. A healthy does of extraverted feeling comes across as empathetic and sincere. Whilst unhealthy dose of if are manipulative and controlling. They usually are very polite and will go out of their way to make sure others aren't embarrassed or hurt and are likely to speak up for other people. Often involved as leaders for social causes such as community work, churches and so on.

Introverted Feeling (Fi):
Creative, bold, quiet, open minded

Introverted feelers tend to navigate the world with a strong system of values and focus on what is right or wrong. If they sense that their value system has been broken significantly enough they will have a strong urge to react. They tend to prefer to express themselves with feelings and actions rather than words. Excellent at listening and coming to conclusions. In life they seek individuality, meaning and authenticity. However they have an open mind to other people's values and believe everyone should be themselves. But they won't tolerate violation of their rights and aren't afraid to stand up for them. Discussing their feelings is difficult and they often privately struggle to be understood. As a result they are often drawn to art and music as a way of expressing themselves.

The Enneagram of Personality

The Enneagram of Personality is a concise way of understanding a person's behavior, based on their dominant characteristics and motivators. It is a model used to represent the human psyche and represents it as nine interconnected personality types.

Knowledge of this is a powerful advantage to reading people. It is widely used in business and social contexts to gain insights into interpersonal dynamics. In addition to increasing self awareness and development.

The Enneagram of Personality can indicate people's motivations for the way they act or think. It can also provide insights into relationships with other people. This will help to identify particular strengths, weaknesses and motivations. In the workplace it can help to manage employees more effectively.

Here are some things to consider about The Enneagram of Personality.

- People do not change personality type
- Descriptions are universally applied to females and males

- People fluctuate between the good and bad traits of their personality type.
- Numbers are used to designate types because they are neutral in value. Large or small numbers have no significance
- No type is worse or better than the other

The Enneagram of Personality

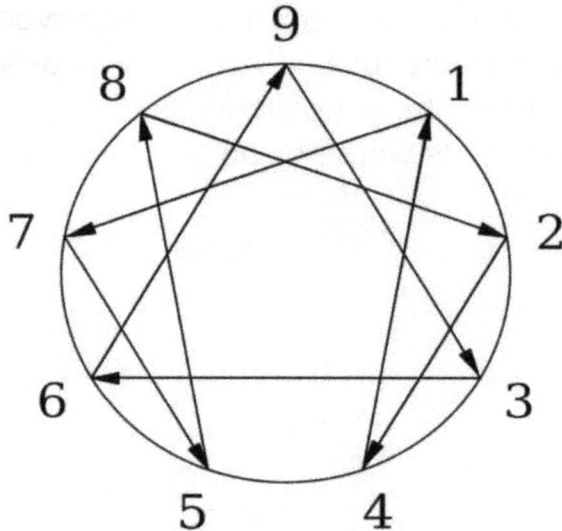

Above is The Enneagram of Personality. It is composed of three parts, an inner triangle (3, 6, 9), an outer circle and a hexagon (1, 4, 2, 8 ,5, 7). The circle is a symbol of unity. The triangle is a symbol of law three and the hexagon is a symbol of law seven.

The nine points around the circumference of The Enneagram of Personality are connected with each other. Each number represents one of the nine distinct personality types. Most of us have a little bit of each of the nine and are more dominant in one of them than others. The one that stands out as being closest to a person is their basic personality type.

To identify someone's basic personality type you need to look at the word clusters for each and choose which they identify closest with. Below are the condensed highlights of each.

Type 1: The Perfectionist
Principled, self controlled, purposeful, perfectionist

The Perfectionist is usually tough on themselves and on other people. They hold everyone, including themselves accountable to higher standards. Normally because of this they are successful and get a lot done in the right way. They want to excel at everything. For them everything has to be perfect and they can sometimes be a control freak.

A strong sense of purpose and internal criticism drives their thoughts and actions. Sometimes they are too self-righteousness and treat others weaknesses with intolerance. However they are dependable and have a lot of self discipline.

Type 2: The Helper
People pleasing, generous, possessive, demonstrative

The Helper is generous, warm, caring and genuinely loves being with other people. They want to be liked. As a result they have many friends who enjoy being around them. They are sensitive to people's needs and are always there to help out. However they also find it hard to say no and as a result are often taken advantage of. This may lead to resentment and bitterness.

Type 3: The Achiever
Adaptable, driven, excelling, image conscious

The Achiever is driven by success and likes to set goals. They tend to excel at everything they do. With others they are charming and inspirational role models. However they fear the opinions of others and try to avoid being low value or low status. As a result they work hard to get the best results and are very efficient. However this can make them a little self centered and oblivious of others feelings.

Type 4: The Individualist
Dramatic, self absorbed, dexpressive, temperamental

The Individualist is self aware, sensitive and experiences emotions on a deeper level. They often spend much time thinking of how things could be. They strive to be unique and are likely to be involved in creative activities. Relationships with them are deep, warm and empathetic.

The challenge for them is frequent bouts of melancholy and self-pity. This can make them emotionally unbalanced and find it hard to work in routine jobs.

Type 5: The Observer
Innovative, perceptive, secretive, isolated

The Observer is a thoughtful and introspective type. They are focused on learning and attaining knowledge.

They are not concerned with status or materialism. Instead they are consumed with searching for themselves and prefer privacy. As a result they often are withdrawn from socializing. In addition they tend to focus on logic and distance from emotion. This can make them come across as cold.

Type 6: The Loyalist
Responsible, anxious, engaging, suspicious

The Loyalist focuses on building relationships of trust. At the outset they can be suspicious of others. Quite often they expect the worst case scenario. This makes them doubtful and in need of constant reassurement in order to make themselves feel safer. As a result they are often anxious and can fall into bouts of paranoia or excessive worrying. However they are dependable and will stick to the rules.

Type 7: The Optimist
Versative, scattered, spontaneous, acquisitive

The Optimist is spontaneous and fun who is often in a happy mood. They are pleasure seekers who avoid negativity at all costs. As a result they are less stressed and don't let negative circumstances bother them. They are always looking for the positive side of everything. This can make it challenging for them to commit to things because at the sign of failure they will jump to the next thing before finishing. This usually manifests in promiscuity, prefering to be free rather than being confined to a monogamous relationship. As a result this can make them come across as shallow and impulsive.

Type 8: The Leader
Decisive, self confident, confrontational, willful

The Leader is a strong and dominant type. They depend on nobody and as a result they make great leaders. They will never hesitate to take over control and utilize their strengths to protect others. This can make them confrontational and blunt at times. Others might be offended by their behaviour even if it was not intended by the leader. As a result they are often misrepresented. This can make them come across as intimidating, selfish and even vindictive.

Type 9: The Mediator
Reassuring, receptive, resigned, complacent

The Mediator is an agreeable and complacent character who avoids confrontations. Instead they love to develop healthy relationships with people. They are non-judgmental which makes them good mediators. However their avoidance of conflict can make them withdrawn at times. As a result many are introverts who prefer solitude and live quiet social lives. This can make them indecisive and easily distracted.

Empathy, The Secret To Easily Reading People

Empathy is the ability to understand what a person is feeling and what makes sense to them. Great communication is founded on empathy. Empathy helps us to communicate and read others better. Prosocial behaviour is considered a sign of empathy whereas a lack of empathy is a sign of anti social behaviour. Having empathy is a powerful way of reading people because it helps in understanding the decision making and thought processes of others.

Psychologists and mental health workers are often experts in this regard and they will have a high level of empathy. People who lack in empathy usually make others feel miserable as they are unable to understand others feelings.

For most of us we are wired to be able to feel the emotions that others are feeling. This explains why we cry during sad movies or laugh when others do. Some of us are more a less sensitive to this. However empathy is a skill that can be trained to be better. Depending on your skill level this will be hard or easy practice.

Signs of empathy	Signs of no empathy
Good listener	Argumentative
Overwhelmed by negativity	Defensive
Sensitive	Strong ego
Intuitive	Leader
Caring	Loyal

Psychologists have defined three forms of empathy which all manifest in different ways. Reflect on your home, work and social experiences to notice the different types.

Cognitive Empathy

Cognitive empathy is the awareness of another's perspective or mental state. It can be further subdivided into the following.

- Perspective Taking: A tendency to quickly adopt the psychological perspectives of others.
- Fantasy: Identification with fictional characters.
- Tactical/Strategic Empathy: Deliberate use of perspective taking as a means to achieve results.

Knowing how another person feels and what they might be thinking on an intellectual level is particularly helpful in negotiating and understanding various views. Rather than responding to another's emotions with the same emotion it is the process of responding to them with brain power.

You don't need to embrace the emotions of a sick person to feel for them. Instead, you can understand the parts of the illness. This is a huge advantage when you need to interact with someone tactfully. Particularly negotiations for which emotions don't serve well. Those who have strong cognitive empathy might come across as cold or detached.

Emotional Empathy

Physically feeling in harmony with the other person as though they have passed their emotions to you. This is particularly helpful in close interpersonal relationships such as coaching and management. In some cases it can be overwhelming because it involves directly feeling the emotions of another. People who are masters of emotional empathy are often referred to as an empath. They have the ability to take on the whole emotional or mental state of another. All humans have mirror neurons to make us capable of this. For example when you feel like crying at a wedding or when you see someone hurt it's a natural response to share their emotions.

Compassionate Empathy

The awareness to respond accordingly to another person's mental state. This is linked to being affected by another person's emotion. It can be further subdivided into the following.

- Empathic Concern: Responding with sympathy and compassion for the suffering of others
- Personal Distress: Responding with discomfort and anxiety to another's suffering. This is a self centered form of empathy. However some might argue that it does not constitute empathy.

Everyone should strive for this kind of empathy, to show love for others and care for their outcomes. This is particularly helpful in healthcare where empathy and compassion is felt for the patients. Feelings of the heart and thoughts are intricately connected. Compassionate Empathy honors that natural connection by considering the feelings and mind state of another person. Some of us will focus more on feeling than fixing.

Development of empathy

Basic psychology tells us that people tend to move away from uncomfortable experiences in their childhood as they grow older. For example picture a child who was always one of the weakest kids in school. Maybe he got picked last for the football team or didn't get picked at all. Over time this person developed a long list of painful experiences and emotions. Psychology tells us that this person will seek to move away from pain as they get older. In practice this means the person is likely to pursue things in life that make them appear strong and not weak. For example they might start lifting weights. Or they might run for a powerful position within the government or another organization. Once we understand that people do things to move away from pain we can get a better understanding for why they do the things they do or act in certain ways. This can help us to better empathize with them.

Let's take a look at another example. Picture a small child named Bill, he grew up on the poor side of town and since his parents report he rarely was able to have nice things. When Bill went to school and saw wealthier kids with nicer cars, phones or other materialistic things he experienced a strong sense of pain. While the other kids enjoyed an amazing lunch Bill was lucky if he had anything to eat. Imagine if this continued to happen in every area of Bill's life growing up and how much pain would build up over time. As Bill got older and gained more opportunities one of his main goals in life whether he realized that or not was to move away from the pain of being poor.

Everyone is born with the ability to feel empathy. Compassion and sympathy are often associated with empathy. Compassion can be defined as the emotion we feel for others in need and it motivates us to help. Sympathy can be defined as the feeling to care for someone who is in need. Empathy is often also compared with altruism, especially in the field of positive psychology. Altruistic behaviour is aimed at benefiting another person. Often when someone is showing empathy with another acts of altruism will occur. All of the above should not be confused with pity which is a feeling towards someone in need of help who they cannot help.

From an early age humans start to display the behaviours of empathy. Toddlers have often displayed concerned for others. Empathic development is greatly influenced by parenting style and relationships. That's why it is a good idea to make sure children benefit from social interaction from an early age.

Females tend to have more empathy than males. Women tend to have more awareness of facial expressions and processing emotions. This is likely the result of females being the primary caretakers of children throughout history. In turn this might have led to neurological evolution that has more empathic responses.

Empathy is not just unique to humans. In fact, some animals have more empathy than humans. Species with a more developed prefrontal cortex often have a greater ability to experience empathy. Rodents and monkeys have been shown to demonstrate prosocial behaviour and empathy for others. Most forms of empathy are built on years of evolution.

Communicating with empathy

Empathy increases with similarities in living conditions and culture. It is more likely to occur when individuals are frequently interacting with each other. The knowledge gained from empathy can help you to use the appropriate nonverbal communication.

- **Understand Yourself:**

To understand the emotions of others you first have to learn to empathize with yourself. Through understanding and accepting your own feelings you can build a solid foundation towards empathy with others.

- **Understand Others**

Practicing and committing to thoughtfulness will bring you closer to understanding how others are thinking and feeling. Interacting with someone becomes easy when you understand what they are thinking or feeling.

Understanding the emotional states of people can be achieved by putting yourself into the shoes of the other. To feel their feelings or understand their beliefs and desires. The ability to do that requires sophisticated imagination which can be trained.

A successful empathic interaction involves accurate recognition of the other person's ongoing emotional states and thought processes. Accurate recognition of those are foundational pillars of empathy. On a basic level humans have the ability to recognize others feelings through body language and facial expressions. Vocal tonality is also a way to tune into empathy.

Individuals acting in an empathetic manner will tend to focus on the long term welfare of others rather than any short term solutions. Empathetic attitudes can be used to improve groups associated with stigma such as the ill, different races, convicts and so on.

Part Two: Clues To Reading People

There are a number of things that you can pay attention to in order to effectively read people. All of us are different but at the core we are the same and everyone gives away clues about themselves all the time. Everytime you interact with people they are sending you clues and signs that you need to watch out and listen for. Awareness of other people's emotions and thoughts will help to improve your interpersonal relationships.

The first step to take is to improve your own self-awareness. However remember don't get that confused with being overly self conscious to the extent that you constantly worry about what others think. That will only lead to base level conversations without depth. Instead try to increase your observational skills and focus your attention onto others. Ideally you want to be looking at everyone without judgement and know when you are having opinions about other people. When you can easily identify your own emotions it will help to reveal what is the driving force of different emotions. Then you can start to predict and see them in other people. In turn this will help you to realize when conversations are going well or not.

Practice makes perfect making predictions about how a conversation is going. When your out and about practice observing conversations. Does that girl like that guy? Who is the leader in the group? Or take the time out and watch a foreign film. Pay close attention to the way the characters interact to see if you can notice anything interesting. After a few movies you'll become a pro at this and your observation skills will become much better. That kind of practice is going to help you become really good at reading people. But the truth of all of this is you have to go out and be scientific about it. Because essentially your predicting patterns and once you start to apply it to your own life it will stick.

That is how you can become much, much better at reading people and learning what triggers them. In turn you can be more captivating and more interesting. You have to get great at noticing the world around you and not the world within you.

Now, let's take a look at some of the clues people give away. Remember to always ask questions that are open ended. This will give you more feedback to analyze and allow you to observe people for longer. Watch out for and listen to their responses.

The Clues

Baseline

Get to know the person you are reading. This will give you a better idea of who they are and how they behave. If you have the opportunity, form opinions of them based on multiple encounters with them.

There are particular mannerisms and habits that everyone has which are unique to them. Everyone has a personal blueprint, showing how they walk, sit, and stand. Establish their baseline. This is their normal relaxed state. Observe how they behave in this state.

To find this out, begin by getting them into a relaxed state. Take the time necessary to create calm, use small talk and low pressure topics or questions. Ask, pause and then observe. Make sure you are posing questions and allowing adequate time for their responses. Try not to overwhelm them with rapid fire questions. Make the questions specific to elicit the kind of information you want. Keep the line of questioning relevant and focused.

Note how they look normally, how they sit, their hand placement, their usual feet position, posture, common facial expressions, head tilt, and even where they place or hold their possessions. Do they take long strides when walking? How do they hold their head? Is their body language open or closed off?

Observe and remember these. When you have an understanding of someone's baseline you will easily notice any differences.

Difference

Once you have established a baseline look for inconsistencies. For example a normally attentive person who seems distracted probably has something going on. Once you understand how they normally behave you will notice things that stick out. Changes in the behaviour of a person signal changes in their thoughts and emotions. Consider when we get bad news, our bodies will reflect that change of emotions. With careful observation we can notice any changes in behaviour.

When there is a different kind of behaviour, it is usually a sign that the line of questioning, stimulus or an event that is troubling the person. Our bodies manifest discomfort in pacifiers. When we are scared, nervous, or uncomfortable this can manifest as fidgeting, touching the face, sweating, breathing heavily and so on. Remember these do not necessarily indicate deception. They could for example indicate that the person is uncomfortable. Liars will often use objects to build a barrier between you and them. This is a sign that they want distance because they are uncomfortable or are being deceitful. Or when people are uncomfortable they tend to lean away.

Determine the cause of the pacifying behaviours. It might not necessarily be that a person is lying but it could be a sign of stress. Go deeper and find the reasons. With effective questioning it is possible to get a better read of people.

Clusters

Always read people in clusters. Behaviours that occur in succession are known as clusters and are the parts of a puzzle to reading people. The more pieces of the puzzle you have then the better chance you have to complete the full picture.

Deciphering singular actions or movements usually doesn't give away much information about a person. But when they happen together with several other movements it will reveal much more about them. Don't jump to conclusions based off of one clue. Take in the whole picture of their, words, tonality, body language and so on. More on that later.

It's important to consider that there is not one way or method that can be applied to every single person. We have to take into account people's culture, family background, environment, mental health and other internal factors. However people do generally follow some patterns in speech, thoughts and body language. These are implicit behaviours such as anxious nail biting, bored foot tapping, avoiding eye contact and so on. Again though try to consider the factors of the person before making assumptions.

Comfort and Discomfort

Observe whether someone is comfortable or not. This is a key indicator to how well an interaction is going. If they are showing signs of being uncomfortable then maybe you need to pull back. Otherwise you can pursue the line of conversation and perhaps go deeper.

People who are comfortable will tend to have more open body language, showing more of their torsos, insides of their arms and legs. A good sign of comfort between people is synchrony in their nonverbal behavior. That is shown in similar breathing rhythm, vocal tonality and body language or posture. On the other hand when people are sitting differently or having different tonality then that is a sign of discomfort

Other signs of discomfort include, a mouth squirming, a frown, an overly long facial expression, rubbing the forehead or neck, squeezing the face, stroking the back of the head, fidgeting and eyelid flutter. If they are noticeably sweating and having trouble to breath then it is an obvious sign of discomfort. Listen to their voice which will likely crack or mumble when someone is in discomfort.

Intuition

Many of us are under the false belief that trusting your instincts is just a cult practice or phenomenon. But there is real science behind it. Emotions originate from the brain and are communicated to our facial and bodily expressions. Those give away so much and intuition picks up on them.

The feelings you have when you first meet someone are usually a powerful indicator of sensing what kind of a person they are. This is your intuition and it is what your gut feels. When you read someone with your intuition it allows you to see deeper than the obvious.

To practice using intuition there are three things that you must pay attention to.

- **Honor your gut feelings**

A gut feeling is your body perceiving information before your brain has the time to think about it. It's a primal response. You can think of it like your internal truth meter and it will help you determine if you can trust a person or not. Be aware of it especially when you first meet someone.

- **Take notice if you get goose bumps**

These are the intuitive tingles that tell you when someone inspires or moves you. Goose bumps are also caused when someone says something that really tugs at your character. It is a positive sign that this person is good for you.

- **Pay close attention to flashes of insight**
If you've ever had an aha moment during a conversation where you felt like you really got a feel for the person's true character then this was your intuition at work. These flashes of insight happen so quickly so they can get lost in the chatter if you're not paying attention to them.

Moving forward there are many, many more clues that we give away in our nonverbal behaviours, our words and even the way we behave online. Let's take a look at those.

Nonverbal Communication

Nonverbal communication is a key indicator to reading people. Most people are unaware of the information they are communicating nonverbally or how to read it. Incidentally over ninety percent of communication is conveyed using non verbals. In fact, it is quite hard to have a successful interaction without nonverbals. This is the reason why people often fly to meetings in the age of, text and emails. Nothing can come close to seeing nonverbals up close and personal.

Body Language

Sometimes the words we say are different from how we really feel. Body language is more difficult to fake. We give off a lot of information through our bodies, mannerisms and gestures. Therefore body language is one of the most trustworthy ways of reading a person.

Body language is the main nonverbal communication and is achieved through gestures, facial expressions, touching, posture, movements, accessories and clothing. Learning to read body language is a valuable skill towards successfully reading people. These can be actions such as eye contact, positioning and more.

Eye Contact

People have always said the eyes are the windows into the soul and if we're talking about a person's true personality then there's a lot of truth to this. Like the entire body itself the eyes transmit powerful electromagnetic energy and if you take the time to observe a person's eyes you can see if they are angry, happy, distracted and more.

When you communicate with someone observe their eye contact. Are they making direct eye contact or are they constantly looking away? A lack of direct eye contact is an indicator of boredom or even deceit. If they look down that can indicate submission or nervousness. Dilated pupils are a great indicator of interest. Our pupils dilate as a result of increased cognitive effort which essentially means more focus on you.

If they glance at something such as the door, that could indicate that they want to leave. Looking upwards or to the left is often a signal of lying. Whereas when people look to the right its coming from imagination.

The rate at which someone blinks is another indicator of how to read people. When blinking rate increases its usually the result of a person being stressed out. In some cases it also indicates lying and it's especially obvious when combined with touching of the face.

Face

When you pay close attention to someone's facial expressions you can pick up on some key non verbal indicators. Specifically, the first thing you should start to do is identifying your own expressions.

Psychological research has concluded that there are six universal facial expressions. These correspond to distinct universal emotions: happiness, sadness, surprise, fear, disgust, anger.

- Happiness: raising of the mouth corners and wrinkling of the eyes. A happy smile fills the whole face.
- Sadness: lowering of the mouth corners, facial features drop.
- Surprise: eyebrows arch, eyes wide open, paler complexion, jaw drop.
- Fear: eyebrows raised, eyes wide open, mouth open
- Disgust: upper lip raised, bridge of nose wrinkled, raised cheeks
- Anger: eyebrows lowered, pressed lips, bulging eyes, flushed complexion.

Pay close attention to the mouth. There are various types of smiling, from the genuine to the fake. Genuine smiles use the whole face and indicate that a person is happy. Fake smiles use only the mouth and are used to seek approval or to establish comfort. Half smiles are usually indicators of sarcasm or uncertainty. A mouth with tight, pursed lips usually is an indicator of displeasure. Whilst a relaxed mouth indicates a more positive and relaxed mood. When someone covers or touches their mouth it may be an indicator of lying or deception.

Finally, the details of a person's face can reveal a lot about their personality. Frown lines on the bridge of the nose or forehead are an indicator of someone who often worries. Whilst wrinkles around the corners of the eyes likely indicate someone more relaxed who smiles and laughs often.

Head Movement

Take note of head movements. When the head moves in harmony upwards with positive statements then this is a sign of congruence in emotion and behaviour. However opposites are more likely to be the result of lies and deception. For example nodding the head upwards when making negative statements.

How quickly or slowly a person nods their head is an indicator of patience. Someone who nods slowly when you talk is indicating patience and a wish for you to continue. Whilst someone who nods quickly when you talk to them is indicating that they want you to hurry up. If they tilt their head to the side when you talk then that can be a sign of interest. Tilting the head backwards can be a sign of suspicion or unease. When people are interested in others they will point their head at them. Take a look at group interactions to determine who is the leader.

Feet

People are often so focused on controlling their facial expressions and upper body positioning that they leak important non verbal messages through their feet. This might sound ridiculous but you can tell a lot about people through their feet. Particularly in hierarchy. When people are in groups you can tell who is the leader by who has the most feet pointed towards them. Or in one on one situations when people have their feet pointed towards you it is an indication of rapport. But if their feet are pointing towards someone else then it's likely they would rather talk to them.

Hands and Arms

Just like the feet the hands also leak important nonverbal cues. Observe where people put their hands. Pockets in hands or touching of head can indicate nervousness or deception. People tend to point their hands towards the person they share the most affinity with. Hands supporting the head with elbows on a table is an indicator of boredom. Hands on hips indicated a sign of exerting dominance. Crossed arms are usually seen as defensive and a closed mind. However with a smile and relaxed demeanor it will indicate confidence and relaxed attitude. When people are holding something whilst communicating it is an indicator of discomfort or unease.

Mirroring

When we are in rapport with someone we often mimic or mirror their emotions and body language. Observing when this happens can give you many clues about how another person is feeling.

Mirroring involves copying the other person's body language, imitating gestures and speech patterns. This can work particularly well in situations such as job interviews or dates. Check to see if the other person is mirroring your behaviour. Change up your body movements and posture and see if they do the same. If someone follows what you do then this is a good sign that they are trying to establish rapport with you.

Mirroring occurs mostly as a subconscious act and often goes unnoticed by both people engaged in communication. Mirroring allows people to feel more connected with whoever they communicate with and establishes better rapport. In conversations listeners will often smile or frown in harmony with the speaker in addition to matching their body posture and movement.

Establishing rapport is an important part of a quality social life. Mirroring can help massively in that regard. This will lead others to believe one is more similar to them and would be a great friend, partner or colleague. In addition mirroring individuals of higher power can create an illusion of higher status. This is particularly advantageous for people that are bargaining with more powerful people.

Proximity

Proximity is the distance between you and the person your communicating with. This can determine if they view you favorably or not. Observe how near or far someone is away from you. When someone stands or sits close to you then it is an indicator of good rapport. However if the rapport is not great they will usually back up or move away from you.

When you see people communicating you can determine a lot about their relationship based on their distance from each other. Although this can also be a cultural thing. Some cultures prefer close proximity whilst others prefer more distance. Always be aware of your location and situation.

Appearance

A person's outer appearance can give away many clues about them.

Clothing

Observe how people dress. Quality of fabrics, brands and styles may reflect status and income level. Logos and fashion choices are good indicators of income. Those who wear fashionable brands are usually on a higher income. Whereas those wearing older generic clothes tend to be on lower incomes. People who constantly follow fashion trends are usually more self conscious and concerned about what others think. T-shirts and attire with other cities and destinations are likely to indicate that the person is well travelled.

A person's shoes can tell you their emotions, political affiliation, income, gender and even age. Expensive shoes tend to belong to high-income earners. Colorful, flashy shoes belong to extroverts. Shoes that aren't new but look spotless belong to conscientious personalities. Functional or practical shoes belong to agreeable people. Ankle boots can be associated with people with an aggressive personality. Shoes that look uncomfortable belong to people with a calm personality. Well-kept and brand new shoes belong to people who often are anxious. Less expensive shoes or flip-flops to belong to liberal thinkers. Plain, boring shoes belong to people who don't care what others think of them and have difficulty forming relationships.

Grooming

A well groomed person is usually conscientious. That would be reflected in a well maintained appearance. Neat hairstyles, trimmed facial hair, ironed and clean clothes. A healthy does of this is normal. Anything less and the person is usually suffering from low self esteem or lower income.

In extreme cases where people pay too much attention to grooming they might well be suffering from obsessive compulsive disorder. In addition, the more people value grooming the higher their ego and income tends to be.

Tattoos and Modifications

Accessories, piercings, tattoos and jewelry can reveal a lot about someone's belief systems, personality, family history, hobbies and interests.

Gang members often have specific tattoos to show their allegiance. People who have been in prison also often have distinctive tattoos. But not all tattoos have negative connotations. They might be related to loved ones or to show a persons artistic side. If someone has a larger tattoo or one in a very noticeable place that usually indicates them as being a nonconformist.

Modifications are things such as piercings, surgery and implants. These also give us important clues about a person. A woman who enhances her breasts will usually do so for confidence reasons. Likewise a man who has liposuccion is trying to increase his value in the sexual marketplace. In the same regard as tattoos the more noticeable the modification the more it gives away about a person. More extreme modifications are often the result of self esteem issues and difficulty relating with people. These people will be more sensitive to communicate with.

Word Clues

The words people say can tell you a lot about them. Choice of words are the result of values, desires, thoughts and concerns. One can get closer to understanding another person by observing the words they speak or write. Behavioral characteristics are revealed through the choice of certain words. Even the way someone texts can reveal many things about their personality.

When we think we use verbs and nouns. Then when speaking, adjectives, adverbs and other grammatical elements are added to turn thoughts into speech or writing. The most basic sentence is constructed with a subject and a verb. For example.

- *"I walked"*
- *"We ate"*
- *"She listened"*

Words added to this structure modify the noun or the action of the verb. It is these modifications that provide key insights into the mind of the speaker or writer.

Using word clues allows us to analyze a person's character. As an example, if someone frequently uses the word "quickly" it would be reasonable to assume that they have a sense of urgency. Conscientious people tend to see themselves as being reliable with a sense of urgency. They might walk "quickly" to avoid being late for work. Or work "quickly" to meet an important deadline. People with this kind of character would make a great employee and this explains the usefulness of listening for word clues. Here are some more examples of word clues.

"I worked hard"
The word "hard" suggests this person values things that are difficult to achieve. It also suggests that they can delay gratification or believe that hard work produces good results.

"I waited patiently"
The use of the word "patiently" suggests this is a person who adheres to social norms and etiquette. They will respect authority follow the rules.

"I love it"
The use of the word "love" suggests this is a person who values family and relationships. They are someone who can be trusted and relied on.

Repetition

Does the person frequently repeat certain words?

"I can't complain about that"
"She makes me happy"
"I'm thrilled to go there"

The above might appear to be quite unrelated statements. However when you look closer you will notice that the word "happy" or one of its synonyms is mentioned in each of the statements. This person is likely to have a positive mindset and will tend to choose things that will make them the most "happy".

When someone is being deceptive they are less likely to use first person pronouns. For example a truthful person might say, "I paid all of the bills", whereas a deceptive one might say "the bills are paid."

People who use "I" more often tend to be more relatable, kind and truthful. Whist those who use "I" at less often tend to be more confident. In addition high status people will use the word "I" the least. People with lower lowest status tends to use the word "I" more often.

Swearing or obscenity significantly increase the persuasiveness of speech and the perceived intensity of the speaker. However it has no effect on their credibility.

A couple's use of the word "we" can predict a satisfying relationship. Use of the word "we" indicates a healthy relationship whereas the use of "you" words suggests problems.

Tonality

Tonality is another important clue to reading people. Consider telephone calls. You can instantly detect the mood of the other person on the telephone. Pay close attention when you listen to someone speak. Is their pitch high or low? How loud do they speak?

There are numerous characteristics of tonality voice that give meaning to a message. These include, timbre, volume, speed, clarity and projection. Different tones can convey different meanings, this can even help in a foreign language. Your tone communicates a lot more than you realized. Essentially, this is the musical notes that your voice communicates separated from your words. Maybe you have a frustrated tone of voice. Maybe you have an angry tone of voice. Maybe you have a warm welcoming tone of voice. Ask yourself. What does this communicate to the people around me? You want to make sure you're sending off the right nonverbals to accompany your words.

A deep voice tone is a sign of maturity and trust in other people. Firm, confident voices convey importance whilst quiet voices convey weakness of uncomfortable. If you want to know who the leader of that group is to listen for the person who speaks with the strongest voice. Some will be loud, some will be very soft but one voice will sound stronger than the rest and this is the leader of the group. This is the easiest way to find a leader of any group and is also a great way to project confidence and become the leader.

The next time that you're walking through the mall or the store or even when around friends or family consciously pay attention to the strength of each person's voice. A strong voice is a good sign that they probably also have a strong personality. a weak voice is a good sign that they probably have a weak personality.

__Reading People Online__

On a conscious and subconscious level we are constantly judging people. This also occurs online. But in this regard we are judging a prepared set of information that shows people what the user wants them to see about themselves.

A person's interests, relationship status, group membership, photos and written vocabulary can help you form valid impressions of their personality. Usually profiles reveal truths we can't always access from meeting someone in person. This is important because if you like someone based on their social media profile then you will probably like them in real life. Therefore creating an online profile with best portrayal of you for someone to positively judge you is essential.

Social media is a revolutionary way of connecting people who might not meet in the real world. This is of particular benefit to introverted people or those with social anxiety.

Profile Picture

Imagine if you could read a person's personality just by looking at their profile picture on social media. In fact you can discover a lot about a person from their profile picture.

People who score higher for neuroticism tend to have simple photos with less color. These people are also more likely to display a blank expression in their photos. Extroverted individuals usually have a profile picture with other people in it. The images are more likely to be colorful and show the person smiling. If the majority of the pictures you post are of you alone then you might come off as conceited. People who have the best-looking profile pictures are most likely to be open to experience and have pictures with a higher contrast. Highly agreeable people are usually smiling and the pictures look lively and bright.

Comments

The way people phrase comments can give away a lot about their personality and the way they treat others. To make sure your making the best impression of yourself say your comments out loud before you post them. Most people are way more harsh online than in the real world. Which can lead to an inaccurate portrayal of them.

Too much negativity can cause our own thinking to be negative and other people's opinions can influence our own. In fact other peoples comments can also influence whether we perceive something as being true or false. When we lack information we are more likely to seek and trust other people's opinions, regardless of accuracy. Numerous studies conclude that when people see more positive posts it influences them to create more positive posts and comments. The same is true with negative posts and comments.

People tend to value receiving comments more highly than likes. Reading comments can even influence how we behave online. That can cause groups or mob like behaviour to form around and idea. Primarily the beginning comment will influence the following negative or positive tone of the comment thread. If it is a positive first comment then positivity will follow. Whilst negative first comments trigger a chain reaction of negativity. On a conscious and subconscious level other people influence and the way we post.

Comments are perceived as social support whilst likes are less personalised. Whereas likes are less personalised and are just a small hit. Most people online users are passive and just consume information without participating. Users who frequently comment on news articles are mostly lower level educated and lower income men. Trolls, or those who frequently post offensive comments tend to have narcissistic, psychopath personalities. Therefore take comments with a grain of salt.

Behaviour varies on platforms. Those where people use their real names are more likely to behave politely. Whereas platforms with anonymity have much more rude comments and personal insults. If your posting very opinionated things then it could damage your reputation. Especially if it is coming from a professional or public account such as Linkedin.

Behaviour

Social media is an extension of human personality. Various studies have determined that social media is connected to a person's mental health, intellect and more. Research has even found that depression is caused by people who frequently browse social media. People who are more self absorbed tend to be more active online, frequently posting and so on. This can directly increase their feelings of importance and confidence. All those likes, follows and shares give a confidence boost that can be addictive. Their values are based on it.

Every time you post something on social media it might be revealing more about you that you want. The way we behave on social media is linked closely to our attachment style, which affects everything from partner selection to relationship development. Recognizing attachment style helps to identify strengths and weaknesses in relationships. It is also a baseline indicator of a person's capacity for intimacy and success in relationships. Those with insecurity in attachment are less likely to be involved in social media and social networks. They may also drive people away.

The big five personality traits in particular, agreeableness, conscientiousness and neuroticism are closely linked with social network addiction. People strong in neuroticism have more chance of being hooked on social media. Whilst conscientiousness people have a decreased chance of being a social media addict. Agreeableness and conscientiousness are also more likely to be addicted to social media. Because friendly, conscientious people will actively spend more time engaging on social media to keep in touch with friends and family to nourish their network. Extroverts are more likely to post about social events and have pictures with people. Those low in agreeableness are likely to gossip about others online.

Presenting a socially desirable and positive self is a natural occurrence for people online. However if your always painting your life to be perfect then you might well push people away. We all have struggles in life and if you don't share them it might well make you not be relatable. If you paint the perfect life it's not really authentic. It might well be as average as the rest of your social media friends. Just give a good mix of the ups and downs to stay relatable. In addition avoid posting too often about every single moment of your life.

Cold Reading

Cold reading is a popular people reading technique used to obtain and imply a knowledge of someone through using high probability guesses. The method works most effectively in one to one communication.

The first step towards a successful cold read is to make sure that the person is compliant. A successful cold read relies on reinforcing assumptions and quickly moving on from wrong assumptions. Depending on the subjects replies dictates whether or not you should pursue further any promising answers or abandon those that are not.

The technique of shotgunning is most commonly used in cold reading. The reader fires a cluster of assumptions and questions in the hope that one or more will hit the target. The subject will reply to confirm or deny information suggested by the reader and this forms the line of communication.

Accurate reads will lead into much deeper territories because the subject will ponder on how the reader could know such things. Expert cold readers emphasize this by hanging on to those successful hits whilst quickly moving on from any misses.

Look out for subtle clues in body language, differences, pacifiers and tonality to determine if a line of enquiry is successful or not. With practice and improved ability to read people, it is possible to quickly read signals and assume whether the cold read is going in the correct direction.

Open ended statements that seem personal yet can apply to many people give the reader a maximum chance of being correct. These statements can be reinterpreted by the subject in a number of ways and will usually make them eager to fill in details or make connections. Essentially they will elicit responses from the subject to correct or provide more accurate responses which reveal a great deal of information to the assumptions.

For example, "I sense you are quite shy with strangers" or "you had an accident involving water when you were a child" or "your having problems with relatives". Or for example, most people wear jewelry related to the loss of a loved one. But if they are asked about it in the context of a cold read then the subject might be shocked that the reader could know that. Successful cold reading makes the reader appear gifted when in reality the statements could fit most people.

Assumptions and statements can also be used to decipher personality traits. Again the reader would present open ended general statements. This is very successful because personality is not quantifiable and nearly everybody has a mix of personality traits. For example "most of the time you are positive and happy" or "your humble and kind person". Cold readers can choose from a variety of personality traits and then use them together with the opposite in order to elicit a response which they can then probe further.

Notable performers such as Derren Brown have openly used cold reading techniques. But only after acclaim and praise did they reveal that their sound knowledge of human psychology was the foundation of their success rather than a connection with the occult.

Part Three: Persuasion and Manipulation

<u>Understanding How Persuasion Influences Reading People</u>

Persuasion is a powerful tool both to influence and read people. It can be directed in a positive way to lead people to take actions that will be of benefit to themselves. This in turn will help to make your interactions much more successful.

The purpose of persuasion is to get attention and spark curiosity. After that it is all about arousing their desire to take certain actions. The key component is in convincing them the value of what you are persuading.

Perception of value differs from one person to the next. But you can create perceived value in something simply by influencing the way people perceive it. For example in medicine, a person must believe that it will heal them in order for it to work. Most of the powerful people in the world are all great at persuading people. They can easily influence and change people's beliefs and ideas.

Supply and demand influences market forces and that is based on perception. When you persuade others to perceive you as the best supplier you can in turn create demand. That is essentially marketing.

The best way to persuade people is to create value for them. The greater their perception of your value the more influence you have. Ethically you can then either sell them something great or something not so great. It all depends on how you persuade them.

First of all you need to understand what kind of stimulation the person you are trying to influence responds most to. Kinesthetic, visual or auditory. Awareness of this will make your persuasion tactics more effective. To determine this listen closely to the way they talk. Do they say things like "sounds good" "I see" or "I feel good about that." Those are some of the more obvious examples or people who are more kinesthetic, visual or auditory.

- **Visual**

Those that conceptualize through visual stimulus
"I see, I could picture that"

- **Auditory**

Those that conceptualize through audio stimulus
"I hear you, listen man"

- **Kinesthetic**

Those that conceptualize through felt stimulus
"I feel, i did"

Adjust the way you persuade depending on the kind of person your dealing with. For example if your dealing with a kinesthetic person focus on how they feel. For a visual person focus on imagery. For an auditory focus on the sounds, and so on.

Persuasive Techniques

Mirroring

A powerful persuasion technique is to mirror the body language, posing and positioning of those you communicate with. Try to be subtle with it at first and practice. It might feel a little bit awkward but this will put you into a better rapport with whoever you communicate with. Particularly in interviews this is a great technique to utilize.

In addition, people respond well to those who use similar language. Pay attention to the words people use and incorporate them into your conversations with them. Also pay attention to their speed volume and pitch. Respond similarly. Mastery of mirroring will go a long way to reading people.

Persuasive Words

A number of words that persuasively influence the subconscious exist. These are often used as a call to action.

For example:

"Do it",
"Be this"

Positive words and adjectives are also persuasive.

For example:
"Sure"
"Definitely",
"Certainly"

In addition the following words suggest urgency.

"Now"
"At the moment"

Be aware of how these can be used to persuade people. You can add emphasis when saying them as a part of your conversations to persuade people subconsciously.

Rhetorical Questions

Convince people that they are the ones making decisions when in fact you steered them to this by asking rhetorical questions. Getting people to think for themselves can be very persuasive. It will also give you more information about them and make them more receptive.

For example:

"You didn't think I would say yes to that, did you?"

"Why not?"
"It's hot today, isn't it?"

Eye Contact

Whenever you're communicating with someone eye contact is extremely important to establishing good rapport. Use consistent and non threatening eye contact and it will help you to develop trust. In turn you can be more persuasive.

Emotions

People respond to emotions rather than logic. In order to persuade someone you need to connect with them on an emotional level. According to the greek philosopher Aristotle there are three elements to a persuasion.

- Logic: Logic words and reasons to your argument. Concerns facts and data.
- Ethics: refers to the credibility, knowledge and stature of the person you are trying to persuade
- Emotion: The emotional content, all non thinking motivations that affect decisions and actions. This is the most important element.

In negotiations persuasion will greatly enhance the likelihood of a successful outcome. Have information about yourself ready in publications and so on. This will give you social proof and make you look more credible.

You might consider the use of persuasion techniques to be immoral or dishonest. However you should be aware of them in order to know when you are being manipulated. Now let's take a look at manipulation...

How To Read and Deal With Manipulation

Have you ever felt controlled, regretful or pressured to do something you were not comfortable with? Or it's like you're continually questioning why you do things for people and have certain relationships? You might feel scared, obligated or guilt tripped into doing something that you don't really want to. If so you might be at the cause of manipulation. In fact you probably aren't even aware of it.

Manipulation is a psychological technique used by people to try to control others in order to get what they want. It exploits mental distortion and emotions in an attempt to seize power, control and privileges at the victim's expense. People who manipulate others are usually doing so because they want to avoid being direct about whatever it is that they want. There are a number of different types of manipulation with some being more obvious than others.

In normal communication there is a give and take to constructive results. Manipulation on the other hand benefits one at the expense of the other in order to serve their agenda. Manipulators are good at reading people and detecting their weaknesses. Then they can convince them to give up something or serve them.

This isn't something that happens as a one time event. In fact, more often than not manipulation is an ongoing process of toxic relationships. Once a manipulator has violated someone they are likely to do it again and again until the victim puts a stop to it.

Manipulation consists of three factors, fear, obligation and guilt. The most common manipulators you will encounter are the bully and the victim.

The Bully

The bully uses aggression and intimidation to control you and make you feel fear. For example someone might challenge your insecurities and confidence by making remarks about your abilities or asking you questions that put you in a negative position. Politicians and celebrities are frequently challenged by the media to put them into negative situations. If your wit isn't sharply developed these quick and deadly attacks can make you look bad and in turn lower your social value. However if you are skilled and fast in this art, the attack can be deflected or be counter attacked to boost your social value.

The Victim

The victim uses guilt to manipulate others and make them feel responsible to stop their suffering. Manipulative people might make you feel like you have done something wrong when in reality you probably have not. This makes the manipulated person question themselves or feel a sense of guilt and or defensiveness.

This kind of manipulation can be very subtle. A person might consistently do a lot of favors for people. However with every favor there is always a string attached. Or some kind of expectation. If you don't return the favor you will be made to feel guilty and look ungrateful. This is an exploitation of the expectation of returning favors and is one of the most common ways that people are manipulated.

It's a standard expectation for us to return favors. Even if someone does so insincerely. This is often why some cultures won't accept gifts from strangers. For example, sales people make is seem like they gave you a great deal as a favor. So you should buy their products to return the favor. Or maybe your colleague bought you a coffee and so you better feel obligated to return the favor.

There are two very common manipulation tactics that are used by manipulators.

Foot in the door

The foot in the door tactic involves someone starts with a small and reasonable request.

"Can I take the afternoon off?"
"Do you have a few minutes to talk?"

This will then lead to a much larger request.

"Can I now take the rest of the month off?"
"You just need $100 invested."

Door in the face

The door in the face technique is the opposite. It starts with someone making a big request. This is very likely to get rejected and then they make a much smaller request. For example someone might ask you for a large amount of money up front. Then when you decline it they will request a smaller amount. This will appear much more reasonable in comparison.

Dealing with manipulation

Consider if you are being manipulated. Ask yourself if your being treated with respect and if the persons demands are reasonable or not. Ultimately you should consider if you really feel good about the relationship. How you answer these questions will help you to identify whether or not the relationship has any further value for you.

In addition you can also ask those questions back onto the potentially manipulative person. Ask them if it seems reasonable and fair to them. Or ask what will you get out of this. It is a good idea to restate their requests to them in order to gain clarity. When you do this it will show the other person the nature of their requests. This might trigger them to back down or withdraw demands.

If they persist with demands you can use time as a leverage to distance yourself. Simply say something like "let me think about it". Take your time and evaluate the request. Remember that it is your human right to say no if you want to later on. If you remain passive and compliant this will give strength to the manipulator. When you start to stand up for yourself then they will back down.

The way you respond to manipulation will depend on the kind of manipulation you are facing. If you are in abusive manipulative relationships it is better to seek treatment and advice from a trained therapist. Otherwise you should leave any toxic relationships.

Establishing personal boundaries plays an important role in reducing manipulation. You have the right to stand up for yourself and defend yourself. We all deserve to be treated with respect, to express our feelings, wants and to say no. Regardless of feeling guilty it is your right to live according to your own terms and conditions for happiness. Manipulative people will try to take advantage and deprive you of your rights. But you have the authority to take control of your life.

In a case of a manipulative work life scenario try to delay your responses. Take the time to analyze the situation. Even better if you have a second person with you. Voice that you need time to consider. Avoid making decisions there and then. Sometimes it's better to sleep on it. Appearing unintelligent will act as a concealment. Try to think in a logical way and take your emotions out of the decisions.

Always be reading and analyzing people to identify potentially manipulative people. Observe how they behave in different situations and with different people. Of course we all act differently in various situations but manipulative people tend to be more extreme in their behavioural differences. In some cases they could be perfectly polite whilst in others they are harsh and rude. If you notice this kind of erratic behavior do not to get involved with them. Reasons for manipulative behavior can be complex psychological issues that need to be dealt with by experts.

Finally, remember that manipulating people for your own selfish goals will not bring you true happiness. Yes, it can easily make you a rich and powerful person but if you don't have anyone that cares about you who you can be truthful with then you will be forever alone.

Conclusion

Here we are. The way you see people will never be the same. Day to day life will be more of an adventure as you observe the various types of people you come across. Your social circle will widen as you begin to read and understand people better. Predicting the behaviour of people even if you just met them will come to you much more easily. You will probably find that your personal and professional relationships will change dramatically for the better. All of this will lead to a better life in harmony with people around you.

It might be time to move on from certain relationships that you have identified as not adding value to you anymore. Living your best life depends on this. You can know that it is the right choice. You can't change people if they don't want to change but you have the power to walk away. To walk away to better things and open new doors in your life.

Trust yourself when you read people. Voices, faces and bodies don't lie. Your intuition is closest to the truth. With this powerful understanding of reading people you are armed with a greater self awareness, more empathy and social confidence. You will be able to see what is true and what is not.

You need to have a trained and sharp mind in order to understand the words and actions of people on multiple levels. Communication is a multi layered form of conveying messages. You need to be aware of what is really meant and implied. This is a skill that can be practiced and improved upon by analyzing and interacting with the people around you. Take notice of the words people use, observe their body language, try to figure out their values and what it is that drives them. Poker players are masters of this skill. Having the ability to identify who is bluffing and who is not.

Whilst you read people make sure you read yourself objectively. Examine your posture, tonality and how you come across. You always want to be presenting the best version of yourself. Observe how people react to you and ask them for feedback. Good friends will be happy to give you honest feedback if you tell them that you are trying to improve.

All this helps to have successful interactions and to be judged more positively. After your interactions ask yourself, what went well, what didn't and what you can improve upon. Keep a journal of your progress and highlight the things you need to work on. Maybe you need a course on tonality or you could benefit from yoga for your posture or acting classes for expressing yourself and so on. Be self aware and journal to really track that and then excel.

Social intelligence and reading people increases your health. The more socially connected we are the more happy we feel. As a direct result our health improves.

In turn, the better we can become at reading people the more opportunity it will bring us.

This book is not intended to make you a master manipulator that takes advantage of people. Rather it is a way to help you read people and have better interactions. This will help you make better decisions, increase your happiness and improve your relationships. Use the information in this book to help you live your best life.

Power is in the people.

Thanks for Reading!

*What did you think of, **Reading People: Harness the Power Of Personality, Body Language, Influence and Persuasion To Transform Your Work, Relationships & Boost Your Confidence!***

I know you could have picked any number of books to read, but you picked this book and for that I am extremely grateful.

I hope that it added at value and quality to your everyday life. If so, it would be really nice if you could share this book with your friends and family by posting to **Facebook** and **Twitter**.

If you enjoyed this book and found some benefit in reading this, I'd like to hear from you and hope that you could take some time to post a review.

Your feedback and support will help me to greatly improve for future projects and make this book even better.

I want you, the reader, to know that your review is very important and so, if you'd like to leave a review, all you have to do is click here and away you go.

I wish you all the best in your future success!

Darcy Carter

Claim This Now

The Confident New You - Develop Your Confidence and Start Living the Life You Deserve

Do you get lost for words around other people, or do you suffer from social anxiety?

If your confidence is always holding you back from achieving what you really want in your life, or if you have always been super shy with no confidence then read on.

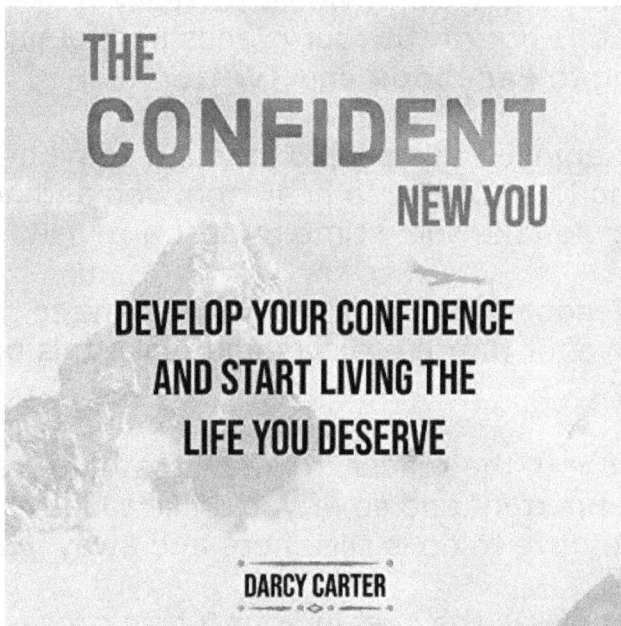

THE
CONFIDENT
NEW YOU

DEVELOP YOUR CONFIDENCE
AND START LIVING THE
LIFE YOU DESERVE

DARCY CARTER

www.ingramcontent.com/pod-product-compliance
Lightning Source LLC
Chambersburg PA
CBHW030259030426
42336CB00009B/446